HOLLYWOOD AT PLAY

The Lives of the Stars Between Takes

DONOVAN BRANDT, MARY MALLORY, AND STEPHEN X. SYLVESTER

Guilford, Connecticut

An imprint of Globe Pequot

Distributed by NATIONAL BOOK NETWORK

British Library Cataloguing in Publication Information available

Library of Congress Cataloging-in-Publication Data available
ISBN 978-1-4930-2720-0 (hardcover)
ISBN 978-1-4930-2721-7 (e-book)

♾™ The paper used in this publication meets the minimum requirements of American National Standard for Information Sciences—Permanence of Paper for Printed Library Materials, ANSI/NISO Z39.48-1992.

CONTENTS

INTRODUCTION AND ACKNOWLEDGMENTS

Hollywood at Play is a celebration of celebrity and simpler times. For decades, movie fans from around the world have been fascinated by classic-era Hollywood (1925–1960) and the larger-than-life stars that gave it personality. Many of those movie fans yearn for the nostalgia of a perceived simpler, more glamorous time that offers a safe and temporary escape from our often complex and angst-filled modern lives.

Nostalgia gives us the major advantage of looking back into the past to highlight the best of times and conveniently overlook the pain and suffering found in every decade. The period in history that this book spans includes the Great Depression, World War II, the Cold War, and the crusade for racial segregation. These were hardly "playful" moments in time. Even the Hollywood Studio system, fondly remembered with a glow of romanticism, had its downsides. In exchange for gainful employment, talent under contract had limited control over their own lives and would be loaned out to rival studios for huge fees that they would never share in.

However, we shall let other books examine the layers of social injustice that encourage the reader to ponder deep thoughts. This book was conceived to encourage the reader to smile!

Hollywood at Play brings to life a time when people had fun without the need for handheld electronic devices and social networks. A time when people seemed more engaged in the moment, person to person, and not so worried with documenting for others a choreographed social life.

Long before social media, people seemed to be more apt at socializing. Even though many of our images were staged for publicity purposes, they are metaphors for how people in the twentieth century escaped from their troubles and tribulations and relaxed with the simple pleasures of bowling, fishing, dancing, and swimming, to name a few.

INTRODUCTION AND ACKNOWLEDGMENTS

We try to capture the innocence of the those days gone by with *Hollywood at Play*, and we have featured unique and rarely seen iconic images of such legendary stars as Audrey Hepburn, Clark Gable, Doris Day, Elizabeth Taylor, Bette Davis, Cary Cooper, Joan Crawford, Cary Grant, Marilyn Monroe, Judy Garland, W. C. Fields, and Tyrone Power being their real selves—not their "reel" selves.

The 127 photos contained in *Hollywood at Play* come from the collection of Eddie Brandt's Saturday Matinee, Hollywood's first and oldest family-owned video store and photo archive.

We hope this book will delight classic movie fans and enthusiasts of celebrity, fashion, popular culture, and Hollywood history, and that the past may give the reader ideas for a new way to play!

Special thanks to Richard Greene, Mike Hawks, Randy Skretvedt, Richard Adkins, Kari E. Johnson, Valerie Yaros, and the Hollywood Heritage Museum for helping to make this book possible.

AT HOME

Screen tough guy Humphrey Bogart plots strategy in a game of chess against his two Scotty dogs, late 1930s. Bogie took his chess seriously, becoming one of Hollywood's best players. He appeared on the Broadway stage with such people as English actor Leslie Howard before hitting it big on-screen in such films as *The Maltese Falcon* (1941), *Casablanca* (1942), and *The Big Sleep* (1946). He received an Oscar as Best Actor for his role in the John Huston film *The African Queen* (1951) and was happily married to actress Lauren Bacall for twelve years.

Leggy Betty Grable interests her black poodle in chasing a ball, mid-1940s. 20th Century Fox insured Grable's legs for $1 million during the height of her singing/dancing career in the 1940s. Those famous gams also appeared as a good luck emblem on many of America's bombers during World War II.

A happy Bette Davis grooms her Scottie dogs, late 1930s. Driven and ambitious, Davis sought out meaty parts in films, rehearsing and practicing skills for months leading up to shoots. She also carved time out of her busy schedule to pose for publicity photos to help introduce her to moviegoers and exhibitors, and to keep her popular with film-going audiences.

Joan Crawford offers treats to her two small white poodles during a relaxing day at home, 1940s. Born Lucille LeSueur in San Antonio, Texas, in 1905, Crawford clawed her way to the top at M-G-M, always ready to reinvent her look to stay popular and newsworthy. She doubled for actress Norma Shearer in the M-G-M film *Lady of the Night* (1925), and only eight films later starred in *Sally, Irene and Mary* (1925). Throughout her days at M-G-M, Crawford would fight Shearer for many challenging roles. She received her only Oscar as Best Actress in 1946 for her starring role in *Mildred Pierce* (1945).

Rock Hudson cooks up a meal at his outdoor barbecue, mid-1950s. Discovered by agent Henry Willson, tall, good-looking Hudson earned an Oscar nomination for playing Jordan "Bick" Benedict Jr. in *Giant* (1956). He romanced Doris Day on-screen in romantic comedies like *Pillow Talk* (1959) and *Lover Come Back* (1961) and Jane Wyman in Douglas Sirk weepies like *Magnificent Obsession* (1954) and *All That Heaven Allows* (1955).

Preparing for a fruit-canning session, Stan Laurel, actress Elena Verdugo, and Oliver Hardy take a break from picking peaches to taste the fruits of their labor at Fort Laurel in October, 1942. Laurel and Hardy were the most beloved and endearing of the movie comedy teams; their immense appeal had as much to do with their off-screen friendship as their on-screen chemistry. Seeking some form of privacy from a prying press and ex-wives, Laurel purchased a one-acre lot at 20213 Strathern Street in rural Canoga Park, California, in 1938. The grounds included an orchard, a vegetable garden, hothouse, vineyard, and duck breeding coop. To secure his privacy, a tall masonry wall, estimated to have been made with one hundred thousand bricks, surrounded the property.

Richard "Dick" Powell and son Richard Powell Jr. take a well-deserved break from working the forty-eight-acre Powell estate with an Allis-Chalmers pedal tractor. Dick Powell was a popular and multitalented American leading man who achieved great screen success as a singer, actor, film producer, and director. The forty-eight-acre Powell estate, later known as Amber Hills, was located at 3100 Mandeville Canyon Road in Los Angeles. It included a quarter-mile, tree-lined driveway, a twelve-thousand-square-foot house, guesthouses, a lake, a tennis court, and views of the Santa Monica Mountains and the Pacific Ocean.

The glamorous Jane Russell strikes a pose for personal pal and photographer Vincent Price. In addition to his illustrious career as an actor, Price was also an expert art collector and consultant, with a degree in art history from Yale University. The Vincent Price Art Museum and Art Museum Foundation are located on the campus of the East Los Angeles College. He was also an accomplished lecturer, author, photographer, and gourmet cook. Jane Russell and Vincent Price became good friends while on the set of RKO's *His Kind of Woman* (1951) and *The Las Vegas Story* (1952).

The California Alligator Farm

THE CALIFORNIA ALLIGATOR FARM
LOS ANGELES

Our Only
SALESROOM
is at the Farm

We make a specialty of Alligator Bags
Ornamented with Genuine Alligator
Heads and Claws

The California Alligator Farm

SEE THE
TRAINED
ALLIGATORS

1000
ON
EXHIBITION

OPEN
EVERY
DAY

One of the most novel and interesting
sights in the world. Most stupendous ag-
gregation of Alligators ever exhibited.

OPPOSITE LINCOLN PARK
LOS ANGELES, -:- CALIFORNIA
Lincoln Park Cars Stop at the Door CAPITOL 2400

Alligator Goods at Wholesale Prices

Ames Bros. Company

HOW TO GET THERE

DRIVING: Go to
Highland avenue and
Franklin and drive 3
blocks west on Frank-
lin to sign indicating
entrance.

STREET CAR: Take
red Pacific Electric
"Hollywood Blvd.
Car," marked
"Gardner," Get off
at Sycamore and
walk 1 block north to
Franklin, where sign
indicates entrance.

SIGHTSEEING
BUSES AND TAXI
will also take you
there — ask the
driver.

Map showing the SCENIC GARDENS and other places of interest in HOLLYWOOD

HOLLYWOOD SCENIC GARDENS AND ORIENTAL PALACE

Franklin, 3 blocks
West of Highland

Fun and Excitement!

THE GREATEST DOLLAR'S WORTH OF FAMILY ENTERTAINMENT IN THE WORLD

World Famous Corriganville Movie Ranch
home of over 2500 Motion Pictures.

SEE
- Fort Apache, Home of Rin-Tin-Tin Series
- Corsican Village, world famous Movie Set.
- Robin Hood Lake and Forest
- Silvertown—an old frontier town
- Circus Tent and Side Show, home of the new television series "Circus Boy"

Restaurant and Chuck Wagons
Horseback Riding ● Stage Coaches
Hay Ride ● Country Auction—most unusual and lots of Fun

A wonderful day in the country — for only a dollar
(children half price)

Come Early and Stay Late –

Give yourself a real vacation — and relaxation.

Only 29 Miles from Hollywood

Just 5 Miles North of
Chatsworth, in the Valley,
on Highway 118

FREE PARKING ● FREE PICNICING

CORRIGANVILLE
SANTA SUZANA PASS
CHATSWORTH
DEVONSHIRE
CANOGA PARK
VAN OWEN ST.
VICTORY BLVD.
VENTURA BLVD.
HOLLYWOOD-FREEWAY FROM L.A.

WORLD'S MOST FAMOUS MOVIE RANCH

Corriganville

EVERYBODY HAS FUN — AT
Corriganville

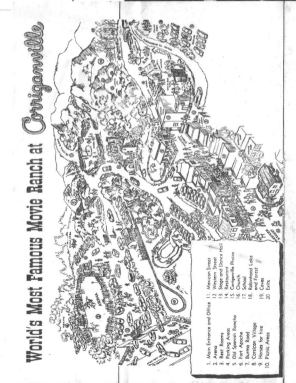

World's Most Famous Movie Ranch at *Corriganville*

1. Main Entrance and Office
2. Arena
3. Rest Rooms
4. Parking Areas
5. Old Spanish Rancho
6. Fort Apache
7. Burma Road
8. Corsican Village
9. Horses for hire
10. Picnic Areas
11. Mexican Street
12. Western Street
13. Stage and Dance Hall
14. Restaurant
15. Corriganville Photos
16. Church
17. School
18. Robinhood Lake and Forest
19. Caves
20. Exits

SATURDAY AND SUNDAY

11:30 a.m. BANK HOLD UP
In famous Silvertown

Spectacular and Exciting
Daringly Realistic

2:00 p.m. STAGE COACH HOLD-UP
In Robin Hood Forest

As you see it in famous
movie scenes.

3:30 p.m. CHAMPIONSHIP RODEO
Thrilling - Excitement
Best in the West

In Person

CHARLEY ALDRIDGE   MAX TERHUNE
BUCK SURESHOT   ENGINEER BILL
JACK McELROY

Plus

Many Famous Movie Stunt Men

While enjoying a leisurely day at home, James Stewart relaxes with a game of pool. Stewart inadvertently helped to hasten the demise of the traditional studio system and forever alter the relationship between the studios and the talent. Universal Studios wanted him to star in two films—a Western, *Winchester '73*, and a comedy, *Harvey*—but balked at Stewart's $200,000 fee. His agent, the legendary Lew Wasserman, brokered a unique deal that gave Stewart no acting fee but rather a percentage of the films' profits and approval of director and cast. With the box-office success of *Winchester '73*, it is estimated that his compensation from that one film totaled $600,000. The end result was a shift of power from the studios to the talent and their agents.

Walt Disney gives an affectionate hug to a young foal, a metaphor for his lifelong love for animals and wildlife. In 1906, when Disney was four, his family moved to his Uncle Roy's farm in Marceline, Missouri. It was on this farm that young Walt developed his love for animals and drawing. He combined his love of both when a neighbor, a retired doctor named "Doc" Sherwood Marceline, paid him to draw pictures of his horse, Rupert. He would forge a lucrative career drawing animals. His first cartoon star was a rabbit named Oswald. And he would go on the create stars out of a duck (Donald), dogs (Pluto and Goofy), an elephant (Dumbo), chipmunks (Chip and Dale), and bear (Winnie the Pooh). He made a superstar out of a common rodent named Mickey Mouse, whose popularity would help finance the Disney Empire

A stunning Elizabeth Taylor shows off the curves that helped to make her an international sex symbol, 1954. Taylor was an actress, businesswoman, and humanitarian. Born in London to American parents, she and her family moved to Los Angeles in 1939, where she was given a film contract by Universal Pictures. Taylor's screen debut was in a minor role in *There's One Born Every Minute* (1942), and the studio terminated her contract after a year. Taylor was then signed by Metro-Goldwyn-Mayer and had her breakthrough role in *National Velvet* (1944), becoming one of the studio's most popular teenage stars.

One of America's favorite teenagers of the 1950s, a radiant Natalie Wood lounges in a hammock, a classic summertime ritual. Wood was an American film and television actress best known for her screen roles in *Miracle on 34th Street* (1947), *Rebel Without a Cause* (1955), *The Searchers* (1956), *Splendor in the Grass* (1961), and *West Side Story* (1961). The product of a stereotypical stage mother, she started her career at the tender age of four.

Lounging in her sun-drenched backyard, the multitalented Debbie Reynolds takes a well-earned rest. At age sixteen Reynolds won the Miss Burbank beauty contest while a student at Burbank High School. That success led to a contract with Warner Bros., but it was at M-G-M where she made most of her defining successes. An avid movie lover, she put a value on Hollywood memorabilia long before others did. Reynolds acquired a stellar movie memorabilia collection, much of it purchased at the heavily publicized auctions of costumes and props from the studios of Metro-Goldwyn-Mayer and 20th Century Fox.

Multitalented Mickey Rooney gets a gentle push into the pool while a delighted Judy Garland, June Preisser, Jackie Cooper, and Ann Rutherford look on. Pool parties were a popular form of entertaining in Hollywood. And a Sunday afternoon pool party at Louis B. Mayer's Santa Monica beach residence was the highlight of many Hollywood stars' weekends. An invite would illustrate your standing within the industry and your ranking within M-G-M. Mickey Rooney reigned as one of Hollywood's top box-office attractions, starring in a series of M-G-M musicals and the Andy Hardy series of family comedies before and during World War II. Judy Garland, "the little girl with the big voice," earned iconic status as Dorothy in M-G-M's classic film, *The Wizard of Oz* (1939). Popular child actor Jackie Cooper gained fame starring opposite Wallace Beery in *The Champ* (1931) before achieving a successful career as a television director.

Happy times for Alan Ladd and son David as they share a playful moment on the diving board of their backyard swimming pool. Alan Ladd enrolled in North Hollywood High School in 1930. Driven by a strong desire to prove himself, he became a high school swimming and diving champion. His swimming and diving skills earned him a role in an aquatic show, *Marinella*. By 1931 he was training for the 1932 Olympics, but an injury put an end to those plans. He later found success as a radio actor, which led to minor parts in movies and his eventual rise to major stardom in the Paramount films of the 1940s.

Dan Duryea tries in vain to share his love of his Lionel 1666 Prairie Steam Engine train set with his less-than-enthusiastic sons, Richard (left) and Peter (right). Dan Duryea was a charter member of that exclusive fraternity of character actors nicknamed "the men you love to hate" by playing superb villains and cads in numerous Westerns and melodramas. He started his career with a Broadway debut in *Dean End* in 1935, and additional stage roles led him to Hollywood. Although made famous for being a slick and wicked bad guy on screen, he was known as a devoted father, a scoutmaster, a member of the PTA, and a gardening aficionado. Peter Duryea would follow in his father's footsteps by becoming a working actor in movies and television, and he later became a dedicated environmentalist. Richard Duryea joined the family's show business tradition as a talent agent.

Actor Glenn Ford and his son, Peter, position the O-gauge Lionel Santa Fe F3 Diesel engine train and railcars atop an elaborately accessorized train set. In 1955 Glenn Ford starred in the critically acclaimed *Blackboard Jungle*, a film set in a gritty New York high school. In a classic example of serendipity, director Richard Brooks happened to be visiting Ford at home to discuss the production, and nine-year-old Peter was playing "Rock around the Clock," Bill Haley & His Comets' hit single, on his turntable. Brooks was so impressed with the recording and the sound of the new generation of youth it represented that he featured the song prominently in the M-G-M movie's opening credits.

The popular actress and dancer Betty Grable escapes from the many demands of her career by enjoying her O-gauge Lionel 1666 Prairie Steam Engine train set. Grable was a top star at 20th Century Fox for more than a decade, starring in many of the studio's lavish Technicolor musical extravaganzas. But being a top box-office attraction comes with a high level of stress attached, and Grable found model railroading a relaxing diversion. Lionel Corporation was an American toy manufacturer of Lionel train sets, which were favorites with model railroaders around the world.

ON THE TOWN

Phyllis Brooks hopes to hit the jackpot playing the slots at gambling mecca Las Vegas, circa 1951, as Cary Grant, Fred MacMurray, and MacMurray's wife, Lillian Lamont, look on with fascination. Las Vegas quickly became a glamorous getaway for stars in the late 1940s thanks to its proximity to Hollywood. Straight-shooting saxophonist MacMurray played in big bands before becoming a film and television star. He displayed a wide range of talent, from portrayals of conniving businessmen in *Double Indemnity* (1944) and *The Apartment* (1960) to kindly widower Steve Douglas in the television series *My Three Sons*. Lamont, his first wife, died tragically in 1953 at the age of forty-five from a heart ailment. Debonair Cary Grant employed his fine comedic timing and dashing good looks to enormous success in such films as *Bringing Up Baby* (1938), *His Girl Friday* (1940), *Notorious* (1946), and *To Catch a Thief* (1955).

Actresses Sophia Loren and Jayne Mansfield get up close and personal during a celebrity dinner in 1958 as an astonished Clifton Webb looks on. In April 1957, Paramount Pictures threw a massive welcome-to-Hollywood celebration for its new star, Loren, at Beverly Hills' elegant Romanoff's restaurant. Bombshell Mansfield hijacked Loren's spotlight to gain a little free publicity for her assets. Loren had appeared in many Italian films before shooting to stardom at the Cannes Film Festival in 1955. Debonair Clifton Webb gained success as a dancer and musical performer in the 1910s and 1920s before appearing in the film noir *Laura* (1944). He co-starred with Loren in *Boy on a Dolphin* (1957). More remembered for her voluptuous figure than her acting, Mansfield starred in *The Girl Can't Help It* (1956) and *Will Success Spoil Rock Hunter?* (1957) before her untimely death in 1967.

W. C. Fields ties one on at Hollywood's scalawag saloon, the Pirate's Den, circa 1941, with the help of a saucy serving wench and co-owner, singer Rudy Vallee. Celebrity stockholders Vallee, Bob Hope, Fred MacMurray, Bing Crosby, Johnny Weissmuller, Tony Martin, Jimmy Fidler, Ken Murray, and Vic Erwin supported their friend Don Dickerman by financing the Pirate's Den, which opened in 1940 at 335 N. La Brea Avenue. Comedian W. C. Fields attended the grand opening of the cafe, which was featured in a RKO 1940 newsreel. Fields's amazing way with words and anarchic personality made him a hit with both stage and screen audiences. He appeared in such films as *It's a Gift* (1934), *David Copperfield* (1935), *The Bank Dick* (1940), and *Never Give a Sucker an Even Break* (1941).

Teenage heartthrob Sandra Dee and her husband Bobby Darin enjoy a swinging night on the town, circa 1962. Immortalized in the song "Look at Me, I'm Sandra Dee" in the film *Grease* (1978), Dee rocketed to stardom in such films as *Gidget* (1959), *A Summer Place* (1959), and *Imitation of Life* (1959). She met her future husband, Darin, in 1960 while filming *Come September* (1961) in Rome, marrying him later that year at the age of eighteen. Singer Darin roared up the charts in the 1950s with such hits as "Splish Splash" and "Mack the Knife," for which he won a Grammy. He died in 1973 at the age of thirty-seven from heart problems.

Hollywood power couples old and new share a toast to future success. Lucille Ball and Desi Arnaz turned their tempestuous relationship into the widely popular television show *I Love Lucy*, in which a daffy Lucy constantly pushed to become a star alongside her Cuban bandleader husband Desi. Ball went on to appear in several other successful sitcoms after she divorced Arnaz. The unsinkable Debbie Reynolds survived divorces, debts, and career downturns as one of Hollywood's most hardworking performers in such films as *Singin' in the Rain* (1952), *Tammy and the Bachelor* (1957), and *The Unsinkable Molly Brown* (1964). She lost her first husband, crooner Eddie Fisher, to glamorous Elizabeth Taylor in 1958. Reynolds and Fisher's daughter Carrie Fisher won fame in her role as Princess Leia in George Lucas's megahit *Star Wars* (1977).

Pirate's Den co-owners Ken Murray and Rudy Vallee savor a little swordplay at their rollicking eatery. Renowned for its crusty sailors, flirty wenches, and potent drinks, the Pirate's Den nightclub's lavish decorations included pirate paraphernalia and jail cells. Vallee introduced many pop standards during his day as a singing bandleader, before starring in such films as *The Palm Beach Story* (1942), *It's in the Bag!* (1945), and *Unfaithfully Yours* (1948). Entertainer Murray grew rich from his Hollywood Home Movies, which Columbia utilized as the short-subject series called Screen Snapshots, before he created his popular stage show *Ken Murray's Blackouts.*

"Hostess with the Mostess" Elsa Maxwell chats up actors Clark Gable and Tyrone Power during one of her elegant parties on the French Riviera in 1948. He-man Clark Gable's rugged good looks and manly charm propelled him to stardom in such films as *It Happened One Night* (1934), *Gone with the Wind* (1939), and *Honky Tonk* (1941). Dashing Tyrone Power followed his namesake father into the movie business in 1925, becoming one of its most handsome and popular leading men in the late 1930s and early 1940s. He starred in such films as *Alexander's Ragtime Band* (1938), *The Mark of Zorro* (1940), and *The Black Swan* (1942) before dying of a heart attack at the age of forty-four after performing a dueling scene with George Sanders in the movie *Solomon and Sheba* (1959).

Gossip columnist Hedda Hopper, Agnes Moorehead, and actor/director Orson Welles enjoy a tête-à-tête under the famous star caricatures at the Hollywood Brown Derby on Vine Street in the 1940s. The second in a Los Angeles chain of restaurants, the Hollywood Brown Derby opened at 1628 North Vine Street in 1929, right in the middle of Hollywood and adjacent to film, television, and radio studios. Open for decades, it was immortalized in an episode of *I Love Lucy* where Lucy (Lucille Ball), Ethel (Vivian Vance), and Fred (William Frawley) dine in a booth with William Holden on one side and Eve Arden on another.

Renowned for her wacky collection of hats, Hopper competed against Louella Parsons for scoops and scandals. She appeared in silent films and early talkies before becoming a columnist. The flippant Moorehead joined Welles's Mercury Theatre on the Air in 1938, performing in the infamous *War of the Worlds* broadcast that Halloween, and she later appeared opposite Welles in such films as *Citizen Kane* (1941), *The Magnificent Ambersons* (1942), and *Journey into Fear* (1943). Multitalented Welles gained national acclaim for directing, writing, and starring in his first feature film, *Citizen Kane*, before top-lining such films as *The Lady from Shanghai* (1947) and *Touch of Evil* (1958).

Attractive but unrelated M-G-M performers Robert Taylor and Elizabeth Taylor share an amusing anecdote, circa 1952, after co-starring in Walter Scott's knight tale, *Ivanhoe* (1952). Suave, sarcastic Robert Taylor starred in such films as *Camille* (1936), *Waterloo Bridge* (1940), and *The Bribe* (1949), and married and divorced screen legend Barbara Stanwyck. Ravishing Elizabeth Taylor won fame as a youngster in *National Velvet* (1944) and never looked back, going on to receive two Best Actress Oscars for her roles in *Butterfield 8* (1960) and *Who's Afraid of Virginia Woolf?* (1966) as well as marrying and divorcing seven husbands, one of them (Richard Burton) twice.

1940s 20th Century Fox leading man Dana Andrews enjoys a meal with ditzy supporting actress Barbara Nichols, early 1950s. President of the Screen Actors Guild from 1963 to 1965 and outspoken advocate in fighting alcohol addiction, the quiet and steady Andrews played thoughtful, sensitive characters in films like *The Ox-Bow Incident* (1943), *Laura* (1944), and *The Best Years of Our Lives* (1946).

Clark Gable and Doris Day make a rare appearance together at the 1957 Academy Awards ceremony at the Pantages Theatre in Hollywood to promote their Paramount Pictures comedy, *Teacher's Pet* (1958). The striking art deco Pantages Theatre, constructed in 1930, hosted five Academy Awards presentations and continues to serve as one of the leading presenters of live theater in Los Angeles. Longtime King of Hollywood, Gable reigned as one of M-G-M Studio's top stars for more than twenty-five years, bringing his rugged masculinity to starring roles in such films as *Test Pilot* (1938), *Gone with the Wind* (1939), *Boom Town* (1940), and *The Misfits* (1961). Former big-band singer Day won hearts playing one of Hollywood's most perfect girls-next-door, starring in such musicals and comedies as *I'll See You in My Dreams* (1951), *Pillow Talk* (1959), and *That Touch of Mink* (1962).

Sultry actress Arlene Dahl and her suave, dapper husband Fernando Lamas enjoy a fancy night out at one of Hollywood's chic nightspots, late 1950s. Mother to hunky Lorenzo Lamas, Dahl starred in such films as *Scene of the Crime* (1949), *Reign of Terror* (1949), and *Three Little Words* (1950). Smart as well as beautiful, Dahl worked as a beauty columnist and writer before establishing her own cosmetics business after leaving the screen. Lamas, her second husband, acted in Argentinian films before being lured to the United States to star in such movies as *The Merry Widow* (1952) and *Dangerous When Wet* (1953). Later in his career he directed for such television series as *The Rookies*, *Starsky & Hutch*, and *House Calls*.

A pensive Jack Benny engages in deep conversation with his wife, Mary Livingstone, and "Oomph Girl" Ann Sheridan at a Hollywood restaurant, circa 1942. Considered one of the all-time great comedians of radio, stage, and screen, especially with his dry one-liners regarding his miserly ways and bad violin playing, Benny starred with sexy comedienne Carole Lombard in Ernst Lubitsch's classic *To Be or Not to Be* (1942) about a ham Polish acting troupe that dupes the Nazis. Benny married Livingstone in 1927 after meeting her in a department store, and she later played his wife on his hit television series. Born Clara Lou Sheridan, earthy Ann Sheridan won a "Search for Beauty" contest in 1932, which led to her film career. She appeared in such movies as *They Drive by Night* (1940), *Kings Row* (1942), and *Woman on the Run* (1950). Sheridan also starred opposite Benny, in *George Washington Slept Here* (1942).

Barbara Stanwyck and her "Golden Boy" William Holden appear together off-camera during the making of their film *Executive Suite* (1954), in which young idealistic Holden views to take over the reins of the Tredway Corporation, owned by Stanwyck's late husband. The two first met during filming of *Golden Boy* (1939), about a man torn between boxing and his love of music, and remained friends for life. Stanwyck lit up the screen playing everything from tough-as-nails dames in *Baby Face* (1933) and *Double Indemnity* (1944) to sexy con artists in *The Lady Eve* (1941) and *Ball of Fire* (1941). Sardonic though serious actor Holden studied at Pasadena Playhouse before breaking into films, appearing in such classics as *Sunset Boulevard* (1950), *Stalag 17* (1953), and *Sabrina* (1954). He served as the best man at Ronald and Nancy Reagan's wedding in 1952.

Wunderkind Orson Welles shares a serious discussion with screen legend Charles Chaplin, circa 1942. A master in many media, Welles formed the Mercury Theatre company with John Houseman in 1937 and created such memorable stage plays as *The Cradle Will Rock*. His imaginative radio presentation of *The War of the Worlds* in 1938 convinced Americans that Martians were invading the United States. Welles achieved screen immortality for writing, directing, and starring in *Citizen Kane* (1941), his first feature film, a thinly veiled portrait of newspaper mogul William Randolph Hearst. Chaplin's Little Tramp character entranced movie audiences in the mid-1910s, becoming one of the most beloved and iconic figures in cinema history. Combining pathos, physical humor, and topical issues, Chaplin's movies such as *The Kid* (1921), *The Gold Rush* (1925), and *City Lights* (1931) delight audiences even today.

Edgar Bergen and Don Ameche look on as Dorothy Lamour plants a big wet kiss on the lips of a cowboy-garbed, horse-riding Charlie McCarthy during an appearance at the Los Angeles Breakfast Club, an institution for decades. Popular ventriloquist Bergen was the voice and brains of carved puppets Charlie McCarthy and Mortimer Snerd, among others. A frequently tuxedo-clad Charlie was the world's most famous ventriloquist dummy, starring in radio and the movies as the wise-cracking co-star to such celebrities as W. C. Fields and Mae West. Ameche launched his career in vaudeville before becoming a popular romantic leading man in 20th Century Fox films. Sultry, sassy Lamour filled out a mean sarong and played a tart-tongued romantic interest to both Bob Hope and Bing Crosby in a series of Paramount *Road to . . .* movies.

Sexy Hollywood superstars Clark Gable and Gary Cooper share some war stories during an evening out, circa 1950. Gable set the screen on fire with such films as *Red Dust* (1932) and *Manhattan Melodrama* (1934) at M-G-M and received the Best Actor Academy Award for his appearance in the Frank Capra film *It Happened One Night* (1934). He later flew combat missions over Europe in World War II before returning to the screen. Sensual, rugged leading man Cooper stole hearts in *The Winning of Barbara Worth* (1926) and never looked back. He starred in such films *A Farewell to Arms* (1932), *Beau Geste* (1939), and *The Pride of the Yankees* (1942), receiving Best Actor Oscars for *Sergeant York* (1941) and *High Noon* (1952).

Tough guys John Garfield and director John Huston discuss their film *We Were Strangers* (1949) while enjoying dinner at one of Hollywood's elegant hot spots. Activist Garfield appeared on the New York stage before being signed to a film contract by Warner Bros. in 1938 and going on to play hard-boiled cynical characters in such films as *The Postman Always Rings Twice* (1946), *Force of Evil* (1948), and *He Ran All the Way* (1951). He helped organize the Hollywood Canteen with Bette Davis to provide free entertainment and dining to servicemen during World War II. Rebellious Huston, the son of renowned actor Walter Huston and father to Anjelica Huston, wrote or directed some of Hollywood's most classic films during his career, including *The Maltese Falcon* (1941), *The Treasure of the Sierra Madre* (1948), and *The African Queen* (1951). He also played the conniving villain Noah Cross in Roman Polanski's iconic film *Chinatown* (1974).

Bette Davis and comedian Jimmy Durante practice a little singing for the 1952 television show *All Star Revue*, a decade after appearing together in the Warner Bros. film *The Man Who Came to Dinner* (1942). Davis received two Academy Awards as Best Actress, for her roles in *Dangerous* (1935) and *Jezebel* (1938), and would briefly serve as the Academy of Motion Picture Arts and Sciences' first woman president in 1941. Famous for his large nose, Durante sang and cracked jokes on stage before appearing in such movies as *Hollywood Party* (1934), *You're in the Army Now* (1941), and *It's a Mad, Mad, Mad, Mad World* (1963). He is widely remembered as narrating the beloved animated television special *Frosty the Snowman* (1969).

NOW! GLEN GRAY and the CASA LOMA Orchestra

HOLLYWOOD **Palladium**
America's Finest
DANCING · DINING
ADMISSION SEVENTY CENTS
(Except Saturdays)

FEATURING
"PEE WEE" HUNT
EUGENIE BAIRD
and the
CASA LOMA QUARTETTE

Charley Foy's SUPPER CLUB

DINNER · COCKTAILS · NO COVER

12915 Ventura Blvd. at Coldwater Canyon
Phone SUnset 1-1482

Presents

TIM AND IRENE
plus
A GRAND CAST

Dine and Dance to Les Barnett's Smooth Rhytms

HOLLYWOOD **Palladium**
World Famous Home of America's
Greatest Dance Orchestras
Hollywood, California

Sunset near Vine Street

Ciro's
8433 SUNSET BLVD.
HOLLYWOOD
HEMPSTEAD 2381

Hollywood Canteen
1451 N. CAHUENGA BLVD.

FLORENTINE GARDENS
Phone HO 6311
5955 HOLLYWOOD BLVD.
HOLLYWOOD, CALIF.

EARL CARROLL
EVERY SEAT RESERVED
NEVER A COVER CHARGE
Dinner Without Dance $1.00
Dance All Evening
Dinner with Lavish Stage Revue $2.50
Phone HOllywood 7101

SPECIAL HALF PRICE TICKET

HOLLYWOOD **Palladium**

L. E. R. C. DANCE CLUB
DANCE
Saturday Evening, November 1st, 1952
FEATURING IN PERSON
GUY MITCHELL
with DICK PEIRCE and His Orchestra

The management reserves the right
to revoke the privilege hereby granted by refunding
the amount indicated.

No. 318

This is not an Admission Ticket—Exchange at any
Box Office for a Half Price Ticket   70c incl. tax.

Make a date with Sugie

YOUR HOST
HARRY M. SUGARMAN
MOTION PICTURE
THEATRE AND CAFE
OPERATOR

Informal DINING ROOMS & COCKTAIL
LOUNGE of the MOTION PICTURE INDUSTRY

Now in the 9th year
EXCELLENT FOOD • EXOTIC DRINKS
ORIGINAL CHINESE FOOD • POPULAR PRICES

BRadshaw 2-2045

DANCING NIGHTLY
IN THE TROPICAL PATIO
IN THE RAIN ROOM

NO COUVERT

IN BEVERLY HILLS — THE ORIGINAL — THE ONLY

TROPICS

421 NORTH RODEO DR.
BEVERLY HILLS CALIF.

The
PARADE OF BIG NAME BANDS
Always a Feature at the

HOLLYWOOD

Palladium

AMERICA'S FINEST DANCING • DINING

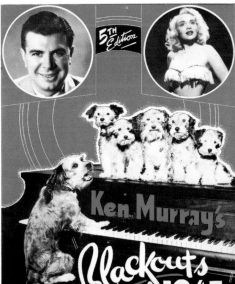

5TH Edition

Ken Murray's

Blackouts

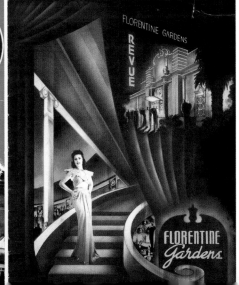

FLORENTINE GARDENS

REVUE

FLORENTINE Gardens

"Mommie Dearest" Joan Crawford gives multitalented Judy Garland and George Burns the evil eye around the time of *A Star Is Born* (1954). Garland achieved immortality after starring in the iconic *The Wizard of Oz* (1939), going on to headline musicals, TV productions, and stage shows with her dramatic singing. Crawford, M-G-M's biggest star for many years, appeared in such films as *Mildred Pierce* (1945), *Johnny Guitar* (1954), and *Whatever Happened to Baby Jane?* (1962). Straight man Burns and his hilarious wife, Gracie Allen, had wowed stage, radio, film, and TV audiences for decades before Burns portrayed the Almighty in *Oh, God!* (1977).

George Raft and Norma Shearer enjoy a night on the town, circa 1939. Shearer reigned as M-G-M's First Lady for many years in the 1930s as wife of studio production chief Irving Thalberg. Shearer starred in such hits as *A Free Soul* (1931), *Marie Antoinette* (1938), and *The Women* (1939). After Thalberg's death, she dated Raft before marrying her second husband, ski instructor Martin Arrouge. Raft earned fame as a hoofer before playing heavies in films like *Scarface* (1932), *They Drive by Night* (1940), and *Some Like It Hot* (1959).

A smiling Maurice Chevalier admires graceful Grace Kelly during an entertainment dinner in the mid-1950s. The charming French singer conquered Hollywood in such early 1930s musicals as *One Hour with You* (1932) and *Love Me Tonight* (1932) before once again stealing hearts in *Gigi* (1958). Philadelphia-born Kelly played glamorous, patrician roles in such films as *Dial M for Murder* (1954), *Rear Window* (1954), and *To Catch a Thief* (1955) before marrying Prince Rainier of Monaco and retiring from the screen.

Hollywood power couples and players share a few drinks at a glamorous nightspot, circa 1939. Left to right: Barbara Stanwyck, Gary Cooper, Errol Flynn, Lili Damita, Veronica "Rocky" Cooper, and Robert Taylor schmooze away from crowds and the cameras, enjoying a little time to relax. Cooper, Flynn, and Taylor enjoyed riding, hunting, and fishing off-screen, when not on horseback for Western and action-adventure roles.

Best Supporting Actress nominee Hattie McDaniel and her escort, F. P. Yober, attend the twelfth annual Academy Awards ceremony at the Ambassador Hotel. McDaniel's performance in *Gone with the Wind* (1939) struck a chord with critics and audiences alike. When she received the Oscar on February 29, 1940, she was the first African American to have been nominated for an Academy Award. She would go on to star on her own network radio program (1947–1952) and television series *Beulah* (1950–1952), in the title role. On January 25, 2006, the US Postal Service issued a first-class Hattie McDaniel stamp in her honor.

Gorgeous couple Tyrone Power and Lana Turner share a look of shocked bemusement while out on the town, circa 1948. Suave, handsome Power, son of the stage and silent-screen actor Tyrone Power Sr., starred in such diverse movies as *Blood and Sand* (1941), *The Razor's Edge* (1946), and *Nightmare Alley* (1947) as one of 20th Century Fox's top 1940s male stars. Rumored to have been discovered sipping a Coke across the street from Hollywood High School, the curvaceous Turner turned heads in such films as *Honky Tonk* (1941), *The Postman Always Rings Twice* (1946), and *The Bad and the Beautiful* (1952).

Luscious Elizabeth Taylor greets screen legend Judy Garland as intense actor Montgomery Clift looks on, circa 1956. Taylor and Clift co-starred opposite each other in *A Place in the Sun* (1951), *Raintree County* (1957), and *Suddenly, Last Summer* (1959), remaining close friends until Clift's untimely death in 1966. Clift emigrated to Hollywood after a successful New York stage career; other films of his include *Red River* (1948), *The Heiress* (1949), and *From Here to Eternity* (1953).

Jane Wyman looks astonished to be sitting between such handsome dinner companions as William Holden and Cary Grant, circa 1959. The first wife of former president Ronald Reagan, Wyman received an Oscar for Best Actress for her role as a deaf-mute in *Johnny Belinda* (1948). She rose from playing sweet ingénue parts to meaty roles in films like *The Lost Weekend* (1945), *Magnificent Obsession* (1954), and *All That Heaven Allows* (1955). Holden received an Academy Award for his role as an American GI in *Stalag 17* (1953), along with being nominated for his roles in *Sunset Boulevard* (1950) and *Network* (1976). Cary Grant never actually received a competitive Oscar, but was awarded an honorary one in 1970 by the Academy of Motion Picture Arts and Sciences.

Groucho Marx and Diana Ross do the hustle during a 1970s-era party. Marx and his brothers Chico, Zeppo, and Harpo wowed audiences with their anarchic humor in 1930s comedies like *Animal Crackers* (1930), *Horse Feathers* (1932), and *Duck Soup* (1933), only to be rediscovered by college students in the 1970s. Diana Ross rose to fame in the 1960s as a founding member and lead singer of the girl group the Supremes before becoming a superstar on her own in the late 1960s. She starred in such films as *Lady Sings the Blues* (1972), *Mahogany* (1975), and *The Wiz* (1978).

Superstars Elizabeth Taylor and Kirk Douglas conquer the dance floor, circa 1960. Virile, steely-eyed Douglas gave charismatic performances in many films, including *The Bad and the Beautiful* (1952), *Lust for Life* (1956), *Paths of Glory* (1957), and *Spartacus* (1960). At Douglas's insistence, screenwriter Douglas Trumbo, a victim of the McCarthy era blacklist, was listed in the credits for *Spartacus*. Taylor conquered Richard Burton, who fell in love with her during the making of *Cleopatra* (1963) and later married her.

Glamorous Audrey Hepburn and legendary funny man Groucho Marx glide around the dance floor at one of several publicity events orchestrated by Paramount Pictures to introduce newcomer Hepburn to Hollywood society and global media. Immediately becoming an international star with her first feature film, *Roman Holiday* (1953) opposite Gregory Peck, Hepburn's European sophisticated elegance provided a sharp contrast to the many buxom Hollywood leading ladies of the 1950s. Wisecracking Groucho Marx starred with his brothers Chico and Harpo in a string of successful 1930s and 1940s film comedies, after touring in vaudeville. He gained even greater fame as the quick-witted host of *You Bet Your Life* on both radio and television.

Janet Leigh and Tony Curtis cozy up a little closer during a romantic ballad by Sammy Davis Jr. at Ciro's nightclub, circa 1955. Opened in January 1940 by *Hollywood Reporter* publisher W. R. Wilkerson, Ciro's immediately became Hollywood's favorite nightclub. Davis gained fame during the Will Mastin Trio's performance at Ciro's in 1951, which launched his recording career. Curtis and Leigh reigned as one of Hollywood's top power couples in the 1950s, appearing in many successful films.

Mickey Rooney and Judy Garland do a little jitterbug after completing shooting on their M-G-M film *Babes in Arms* (1939), which greatly mimicked their own lives. The movie tells the story of two ambitious young people attempting to make it in show business. Rooney, born Joe Yule Jr., worked in vaudeville as a tot and earned rave reviews for his performance in the Colleen Moore silent film *Orchids and Ermine* (1927), changing his name to that of the character, Mickey McGuire. He would go on to star in a Mickey McGuire short series before becoming one of M-G-M's top male stars in the 1930s and 1940s and appearing with Judy Garland in a series of musicals.

It's "Hollywood Night at the Fights" as Bruce Cabot, Jack Oakie and his wife Venita Varden, Randolph Scott, and Cary Grant enjoy some fisticuffs, late 1930s. Scott and Grant appeared in two films together, *Hot Saturday* (1932) and *My Favorite Wife* (1940), competing for the hand of the leading lady. The dashing Grant starred in four Alfred Hitchcock thrillers opposite lovely blondes, including *Suspicion* (1941), *Notorious* (1946), *To Catch a Thief* (1955), and *North by Northwest* (1959). Scott got his start in romantic comedies during the 1930s before playing uncompromising, hard-bitten men in Westerns. Known for his joking manner and triple take talent, Oakie is probably best remembered for his role in Charlie Chaplin's *The Great Dictator* (1940).

Jack Benny, Barbara Stanwyck, and Robert Taylor attend one of Los Angeles's many boxing matches, late 1930s. Comedian Benny succeeded in stage, radio, films, and television thanks to his dry, self-deprecating sense of humor and amusing interplay with his co-stars. Hard-working, versatile Stanwyck and her handsome, four years younger husband Taylor enjoyed the great outdoors at their Northridge Ranch for thirteen years before divorcing in 1952.

Jeanne Crain and husband Paul Brinkman pause to pose for the camera as they step out for a night on the town. As a teenager in the early 1940s, Crain won the title of Miss Pan-Pacific at the Los Angeles Pan-Pacific Auditorium. Her movie career began while under contract to 20th Century Fox and she would go on to star in many of the studio's box-office hits from 1945 to 1953. Earning the nickname of "Hollywood's Number One Party Girl," she was escorted to parties by her future husband Brinkman, aka Paul Brooks, a former RKO Pictures contract player.

ON THE SET

Perky young Audrey Hepburn scoots around the Paramount Pictures backlot on a World bicycle while in costume for the 1954 film *Sabrina*. Her cool beauty and classy elegance epitomize style and grace to this day. Hepburn received an Oscar for Best Actress for her first American film *Roman Holiday* in 1953, before starring in such classic films as *Sabrina* (1954), *Funny Face* (1957), and *Breakfast at Tiffany's* (1961).

ON THE SET

Voluptuous Ann-Margret steers her moped with her shapely legs as she hangs ten on the bike, circa 1964. The Swedish sex symbol gained fame in musicals such as *State Fair* (1962) and *Bye Bye Birdie* (1963) before burning up the screen in *Viva Las Vegas* (1964) with Elvis Presley, and *Kitten with a Whip* (1964). She later starred in such films as *Carnal Knowledge* (1971) and *Tommy* (1975).

Trying to stay limber and loose, athletic Clint Eastwood performs a handstand while on a break from his role as Rowdy Yates in the television show *Rawhide*, circa 1960. Tough-as-nails Eastwood gained fame in television before portraying macho "men with no name" in such spaghetti westerns as *A Fistful of Dollars* (1964), *For a Few Dollars More* (1965), and *The Good, the Bad and the Ugly* (1966), and mad-as-hell San Francisco police inspector Harry Callahan in a series of films. He has received two Oscars for directing: *Unforgiven* (1992) and *Million Dollar Baby* (2004).

Jack Lemmon, James Cagney, and wives Cynthia Stone and Frances Cagney relax at a Hawaiian luau during the making of the film *Mister Roberts* (1955). Accomplished jazz pianist and raconteur Lemmon embodied anxiety-ridden, nervous company men in such films as *The Apartment* (1960), *Save the Tiger* (1973), and *China Syndrome* (1979), while also letting loose his feminine side in *Some Like It Hot* (1959). Kinetic, magnetic Cagney leaped off the screen in such powerful movies as *The Public Enemy* (1931), *Yankee Doodle Dandy* (1942), and *White Heat* (1949).

Phyllis Kirk dances with Robby the Robot during a break in filming an episode of the television series *The Thin Man* in 1958, in which they investigate whether a robot could have been employed in a murder. Japanese-American art director Robert Kinoshita created Robby in 1955 for $125,000 for the M-G-M sci-fi film *Forbidden Planet*. Robby appeared in twenty-five films and television shows, mostly with science fiction backgrounds. Kirk starred as Nora Charles opposite Peter Lawford in the 1950s M-G-M TV series *The Thin Man*, based on the series of films produced by the studio in the 1930s and 1940s.

A badge of his early success, Matthew "Stymie" Beard Jr. of the *Our Gang* comedy shorts proudly shows off a pint-sized custom roadster. *Our Gang* director Robert McGowan gave five-year-old Matthew Beard Jr. his nickname after constantly having to search for Matthew when the cameras were ready to roll at the Hal Roach studios. This game of hide-and-seek "stymied" (to prevent or hinder progress) filming. Despite the frustration caused on the set, Stymie was the favorite "gang" member of series director McGowan.

ON THE SET

Dean Martin as Matt Helm prepares to hang on for a ride with a movie extra on a Vespa scooter on the set of *The Ambushers* (1967). For over three decades, Dean Martin reigned as one of America's most popular and enduring entertainers, with an appeal that spawned multiple generations. Despite a successful career recording records, headlining in Las Vegas, a hit television show, and movie stardom, Martin found time to star in four Matt Helm based films, *The Silencers* (1966), *Murderers' Row* (1966), *The Ambushers* (1967), and *The Wrecking Crew* (1969).

James Coburn (in sidecar), James Garner, and Steve McQueen pose with director/producer John Sturges, before embarking on a three-wheeled cruise during a break in filming *The Great Escape* (1963). Actor McQueen reached his superstar status with the release of *The Great Escape*, the story of a daring and methodically planned WWII prison break. His love for motorcycles was a big motivator behind the scene of his famous motorcycle escape from a German POW camp. With the Nazis in hot pursuit, the chase includes a harrowing motorcycle jump over a barbed wire fence by stunt performer Bud Ekins, not McQueen, because the risk of injury to the top star was too great.

James MacArthur takes his adoptive mother, Helen Hayes, for a ride on his Vespa scooter around the Desilu Studio lot in Culver City, 1959. Helen Hayes's long and distinguished stage career earned her the nickname "First Lady of American Theater." Her acclaim as an actress made her one of only twelve people to have been awarded an Emmy, a Grammy, an Oscar, and a Tony (the elusive "EGOT"). In 1986 Hayes received from President Ronald Reagan America's highest civilian honor, the Presidential Medal of Freedom. MacArthur would go on to follow in the family acting tradition. Outstanding performances on television and critically acclaimed roles in motion pictures would cement his image as an intelligent and sensitive young leading man. His greatest acting success came several years later when he was cast as detective Danny Williams on the long-running police drama *Hawaii 5-0.*

ON THE SET

Montgomery Clift lines up a pool shot during a break on the set of *From Here to Eternity* (1953). "Monty" Clift was a film and stage actor best known for his portrayal of moody, complicated, and sensitive young men. His skills as an actor earned him four Academy Award nominations during his distinguished career, three for Best Actor in *The Search* (1948), *A Place in the Sun* (1951), *From Here to Eternity* (1953), and one for Best Supporting Actor in *Judgment at Nuremberg* (1961).

Ernie Kovacs lines up a shot during a game of pool with Lucille Ball while filming an episode of *The Lucy-Desi Comedy Hour*, 1960. When the demands of a weekly sitcom series became too much for Lucille Ball and husband Desi Arnaz, the practical compromise was *The Lucy-Desi Comedy Hour*, which aired periodically from 1957 to 1960 on CBS. In the final episode, "Lucy Meets the Moustache," Kovacs and Edie Adams move in next door to the Ricardos' Westport, Connecticut, home. The story revolves around Lucy's attempts to get husband Ricky a spot on an upcoming Kovacs television special. Sadly, when work on this episode ended, Ball filed for divorce from Arnaz, ending their twenty-year marriage.

Actors Leslie Howard, Reginald Denny, and John Barrymore marvel at the "Denny Jr." model airplane on the backlot set of M-G-M's *Romeo and Juliet* (1936). Along with a successful acting career, the English-born Denny was also known for his interest in aviation. Denny turned his aviation passion into a successful business venture, forming Reginald Denny Industries in 1934. One of his popular models, the Denny Jr., was featured prominently in the Jane Withers movie *The Holy Terror* (1937). The Denny model planes were available for purchase at his famous Hollywood store, Reginald Denny's Hobby Shop, at 5751 Hollywood Boulevard.

The AMBASSADOR

*a world famous hotel crowning
its 22 acre park in the heart of
the smart Wilshire district at*

LOS ANGELES, CALIFORNIA

*a world famous hotel crowning
its 22 acre park in the heart of
the smart Wilshire district at*

LOS ANGELES, CALIFORNIA

*The great Hotel that
seems like Home*

*Center for the social life of
Los Angeles and Hollywood*

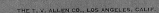

The HOLLYWOOD PLAZA HOTEL

The HOLLYWOOD PLAZA HOTEL

PALM GROVE

A Tropical Garden Room with that modern touch. Dine and enjoy yourself in an atmosphere depicting the charm and gay life of Old Mexico. The only one of its kind in the heart of Hollywood.

THE CINNABAR RESTAURANT

At the brilliant premiere, Moviedom gasped with admiration of its gorgeous beauty. The novelty of design, the richness of coloring and the elegance of the furnishings defy description. Its equal is not to be seen in Hollywood's galaxy of splendor. The main features of this spacious Restaurant are the heroic Movie Murals, all different, and each framed by wide sculptured frames of rich Cinnabar red. Your Hollywood trip is not complete without a visit to this amazing CINNABAR Restaurant with its delicious food and popular prices.

HOLLYWOOD PLAZA RATES

Single	. . .	From $3.00
Double	. . .	From $4.50
Suites	. . .	From $8.00

THE HOLLYWOOD PLAZA HOTEL

A HULL Hotel

Thomas E. Hull, Managing Director

Vine Street at Hollywood Boulevard

Gladstone 1131

and Cinnabar Restaurant

IN THE HEART OF HOLLYWOOD

Lon Chaney Jr.'s German Shepherd "Moose" would rather go for a walk than study the script for his part as the wolf Bruno on the set of *The Wolf Man* (1941). Creighton Tull Chaney, aka Lon Chaney Jr., was the son of legendary actor Lon Chaney, known around the world as "The Man of a Thousand Faces." *The Wolf Man* was originally intended to be a project for Universal's big star Boris Karloff, but the movie's success made Chaney Jr. the new king of the studio's horror films. Aside from Chaney's performance, much of the popularity of that film can also be credited to Universal makeup artist Jack P. Pierce, who created the Wolf Man's convincing signature look using a rubber nose and singed yak hair glued in place with spirit gum.

ON THE SET

Frequent co-stars and friends Harry Belafonte and Dorothy Dandridge share a smile on the set of *Carmen Jones* (1954). After seeing Dandridge sing at the Mocambo, a famous Sunset Boulevard nightclub, in December 1952, Metro-Goldwyn-Mayer cast her as Jane Richards in *Bright Road* (1953). It would be Dandridge's first film appearance opposite Harry Belafonte, who was making his feature-film debut. Their second film together, the musical extravaganza *Carmen Jones,* became an international success, eventually earning over $10 million at the box office and becoming one of the year's highest-earning films.

Dean Martin, Jerry Lewis, Bob Hope, Meredith Willson, Louie Armstrong, Frankie Laine, show host Tallulah Bankhead, and Deborah Kerr share a laugh during a rehearsal for the *Big Show* radio program on December 17, 1950. *The Big Show* was a ninety-minute NBC radio variety program featuring the biggest names in show business. The big-budgeted show was developed with the goal of enabling the established medium of radio to successfully compete against the exciting new medium of television. *The Big Show* was performed at and broadcast from the streamlined Modern Hollywood Studios of NBC at Sunset and Vine.

Bela Lugosi hams it up during a publicity shoot to promote what came to be titled *Bela Lugosi Meets a Brooklyn Gorilla* (1952). Jack Broder, an independent producer, offered Lugosi a major role in the low-budget, jungle-themed comedy. The film co-starred 1950s nightclub comedians Duke Mitchell and Sammy Petrillo, with actor Steve Calvert in the gorilla suit. Filming took place at Hollywood's original General Service Studios with a nine-day shooting schedule and a budget of $50,000.

Classic horror film titans Boris Karloff and Bela Lugosi play a game of chess during a scene from *The Black Cat*, Universal's biggest hit of 1934. It was the first film to pair Lugosi and Karloff, the two biggest stars of horror films. Part of the appeal of *The Black Cat* is the unique and dazzling art direction of Charles D. Hall, a Universal art director from 1923 to 1937. Although they did not socialize, Karloff and Lugosi had a cordial and professional working relationship, contrary to the unfounded and exaggerated rumors circulated by the press. The pair would go on to make seven more films together, with Karloff always securing top billing.

A young Ronny Howard takes a break from schoolwork with younger brother Clint. Ron Howard was born in Duncan, Oklahoma, the son of show business parents. The family moved to Hollywood in 1958. In 1960, Howard was cast as Opie Taylor in *The Andy Griffith Show*, and he portrayed the son of Andy Griffith for all eight seasons of the show's run on CBS. Clint Howard began his career when he was two, appearing in five episodes of *The Andy Griffith Show*. He played Leon, a toddler in a cowboy outfit who wandered around Mayberry and silently offered people a bite of his sandwich.

A playful Peter O'Toole and Hugh O'Brian get the draw on Sammy Davis Jr. after attending a performance of *Golden Boy* at Broadway's Majestic Theater in 1965. *Golden Boy* was a 1964 musical version of a 1937 drama set in the world of professional boxing. The original play was written by Clifford Odets; it was updated by William Gibson, with lyrics by Lee Adams and music by Charles Strouse. The production, starring Sammy Davis Jr., was nominated for four Tony Awards: Best Choreography, Best Musical, Best Actor in a Musical (Davis), and Best Producer of a Musical.

Boris Karloff is poised to throw a forward pass with a life-size bust of an old acquaintance, the Frankenstein monster, during a break while filming the television series *Thriller*. As host of the anthology television series, Karloff would introduce a mix of stories that featured macabre tales of horror and suspenseful thrillers with an impressive list of guest stars. Beyond his role of host, Karloff starred in five episodes of *Thriller*: "The Prediction," "The Premature Burial," "The Last of the Sommervilles," "Dialogues with Death," and "The Incredible Doctor Markesan."

On the set of *Beyond the Purple Hills* (1950), Gene Autry delights in the roping skills of a young and talented cowboy fan. Autry's fans had many options to see their Western hero on-screen and in print. However, it was most thrilling to see him perform in person in his traveling rodeo. In the mid-1930s Autry began touring in a small Western show, playing one-night stands in between film commitments. By 1939, an expanded Gene Autry Rodeo started playing larger venues, from county and state fairs to New York's Madison Square Garden.

Charlie McCarthy takes perverse pleasure in the hanging of a "dummy" version of his archrival, comedian W. C. Fields. Charlie McCarthy was the creation and alter ego of actor, comedian, and ventriloquist Edgar Bergen. Together they starred on *The Chase and Sanborn Hour*, an NBC radio success from 1937 to 1956. Bergen's talented voice characterization and comic timing brought Charlie McCarthy to life for listeners; many considered the large wooden doll to be a real-life performer. Charlie, with his signature top hat, cape, and monocle could get away with the risqué one-liners that Bergen could not. Charlie's comedic feud with Fields was a regular feature of the show and an audience favorite.

Errol Flynn and Olivia de Havilland thrust and parried back and forth during a break from filming *The Adventures of Robin Hood* (1938). Flynn became big box office straight out of the gate with his first starring Hollywood role, *Captain Blood* (1935) and went on to be typecast as an athletic swashbuckler in a series of action-adventure films. The success of *The Adventures of Robin Hood* gave a big boost to de Havilland's career as well. The pair had a screen chemistry that would last through a total of nine movies.

Cary Grant and Doris Day take a pool break at the Fairmont Miramar Hotel in Santa Monica during the filming of *That Touch of Mink* (1962). Originally the site of a private mansion owned by John P. Jones, the founder of Santa Monica and a former US senator, the Fairmont Miramar Hotel has served as an exclusive playground for the Hollywood crowd since 1921. A modern ten-story tower and the pool featured in the film were built on the property during a renovation in 1959. While playing at New York's Radio City Music Hall, *That Touch of Mink* was the first film in movie history to gross $1 million in one theater.

THE SPORTING LIFE

Hollywood loved America's favorite pastime, rooting for local baseball teams the Los Angeles Angels, the Hollywood Stars, and the Los Angeles Dodgers at Wrigley Field, Gilmore Field, and Dodger Stadium, during time off. Stars often suited up for charity games, such as the one pictured here, circa 1960. Scream queen Janet Leigh cheers on her charity team, including from left to right, Peter Lawford, trumpeter Harry James, unidentified, Jeff Chandler, and Hugh O'Brian.

Boris Karloff as Frankenstein's monster swings for a strike during a Hollywood Stars charity baseball game at Gilmore Field, the current site of CBS Television City and the Grove at the Farmers Market in Los Angeles. Many a celebrity played baseball, aping the real boys of summer, on this field, home of the Pacific Coast League Stars. Comedian Buster Keaton, another avid baseball fan, is behind home plate wearing the catcher's mask.

Hoboken, New Jersey's most famous resident, crooner Frank Sinatra, plays a little catch with the guys on the street of his hometown, mid-1940s. One of the all-time great singers and founder of the swinging '60s "Rat Pack," Sinatra rose from saloon singer to soloist in Harry James's and Tommy Dorsey's big bands before becoming a major movie star. Beside selling more than 150 million records for his smooth recordings of tunes from the Great American Songbook, Sinatra received the Academy Award for Best Supporting Actor for his portrayal of Private Angelo Maggio in Fred Zinnemann's *From Here to Eternity* (1953).

Champion bowler and trick shot artist Andy Varipapa strikes a pose with ten shapely showgirls for Pete Smith's Metro-Goldwyn-Mayer short *Strikes and Spares* (1934). The leggy lasses served as live bowling pins as Varipapa rolled a trick shot between all their legs for one scene in the film, later nominated for a Best Short Subject, Novelty, Academy Award. Varipapa later starred in two other bowling short films for M-G-M and Smith: *Set 'em Up* (1939) and *Bowling Tricks* (1948).

English rose Joan Fontaine enjoys a little bowling in her spare time, early 1940s. Especially after World War II, bowling became one of America's most popular family pastimes, a relatively inexpensive way to enjoy time together. Fontaine received an Oscar as Best Actress for her role in the Alfred Hitchcock film *Suspicion* (1941), and starred in such films as *Rebecca* (1940), *Letter from an Unknown Woman* (1948), and *Born to Be Bad* (1950). Fontaine was long estranged from her Academy Award–winning sister, actress Olivia de Havilland, before dying in 2013.

Charles Winninger slips and falls during a rowdy bowling competition with *Beyond Tomorrow* co-stars C. Aubrey Smith, Harry Carey, and Maria Ouspenskaya. A veteran of the vaudeville and Broadway stages, Winninger originated the role of Cap'n Andy in *Show Boat* on Broadway in 1927. He appeared in such films as *Three Smart Girls* (1936), *Nothing Sacred* (1937), and *Destry Rides Again* (1939). Britisher Smith brought a stern stiff upper lip to such American films as *The Garden of Allah* (1936), *The Prisoner of Zenda* (1937), *Rebecca* (1940), and *Waterloo Bridge* (1940). Carey gained fame in Westerns before starring in such films as *Trader Horn* (1931), *The Prisoner of Shark Island* (1936), and *Mr. Smith Goes to Washington* (1939). Russian Ouspenskaya joined the Moscow Art Theatre before defecting to the United States and appearing on Broadway. Her film roles include *Dodsworth* (1936), *Love Affair* (1939), and *The Wolf Man* (1941).

Fun-loving actress Carole Lombard enjoys a leisurely game of bowling in high heels, mid-1930s. Gaining experience in small comedic roles for Fox Films and the Mack Sennett Studios, Lombard went on to star in such movies as *Twentieth Century* (1934), *My Man Godfrey* (1936), and *Nothing Sacred* (1937). Known as much for her happy-go-lucky personality as her profane mouth, Lombard married the love of her life Clark Gable before dying tragically at the age of thirty-three in an airplane crash when returning from a World War II war bond rally.

Barbara Eden strikes a pose in her spare time at the local bowling alley. Best known for her memorable role as Larry Hagman's adoring, zany genie in the 1960s TV sitcom, *I Dream of Jeannie*, Eden has appeared in many films and TV shows, including *Voyage to the Bottom of the Sea* (1961), *7 Faces of Dr. Lao* (1964), and *Harper Valley P.T.A.* (1978).

A pleased Warner Baxter shows off his prizewinning catch after a day of fly-fishing, mid-1930s. A popular leading man for decades, Baxter starred as Jay Gatsby in the original *The Great Gatsby* (1926), and would star opposite Dolores Del Rio in *Ramona* (1928), Myrna Loy in *Penthouse* (1933), and Alice Faye in *The King of Burlesque* (1936).

Amanda Blake of *Gunsmoke* fame gets in a little fishing between acting gigs in the 1950s. Best known for her role as the steadfast madam Miss Kitty in the long-running television series *Gunsmoke* (1955–1974) opposite series regulars James Arness, Milburn Stone, and Ken Curtis, Blake began her career playing second-lead parts in such films as *Duchess of Idaho* (1950), *Lili* (1953), and *About Mrs. Leslie* (1954).

Good-girl Doris Day helps Rock Hudson get into the swing of things playing golf for the film *Lover Come Back* (1961). Bubbly animal lover Day began her show business career as a big-band singer with Les Brown's Band of Renown before jumping into movies in the late 1940s. Her fine singing, comic timing, and vulnerable personality brought her fame in such films as *Calamity Jane* (1953), *Love Me or Leave Me* (1955), and *The Man Who Knew Too Much* (1956). Hudson's likable persona and comic flair played well against prim and proper Day.

Crooner Bing Crosby parades his way to the first tee at the "Crosby Clambake," the National Pro-Am Golf Championship at Pebble Beach, circa 1950. Pebble Beach Golf Links, along 17-Mile Drive between Carmel and Monterey, is considered one of the world's most beautiful golf courses, hosting PGA championships and US Opens throughout its history. Gaining fame as a singer with such performers as Paul Whiteman, Bix Beiderbecke, Tommy and Jimmy Dorsey, and Hoagy Carmichael, Crosby soared to the top of the charts both in music and film, recording one of the top-selling songs of all time, *White Christmas*, as well as receiving an Academy Award for Best Actor in *Going My Way* (1944).

Silent film actress Mae Murray checks for the "all clear" before hitting her golf shot at a Northern California golf course, mid-1920s. A headlining dancer in New York before becoming a film star in Hollywood in such films as Erich von Stroheim's *The Merry Widow* (1925), Murray earned the nickname "The Girl with the Bee-Stung Lips" thanks to her small, pouty mouth. Her extravagant costumes, exaggerated acting, and over-the-top personality eventually doomed her acting career.

Voluptuous Mamie Van Doren shows off her form in the golf course rough, late 1950s. More famous for her figure than her acting talent, buxom Van Doren appeared in rock 'n' roll and exploitation films that amply displayed her physical assets like *High School Confidential!* (1958), *The Beat Generation* (1959), and *Sex Kittens Go to College* (1960).

Robert Taylor practices chipping a few golf balls in the backyard of his home, mid-1950s. Taylor began his career playing attractive romantic leads in such films as *Camille* (1936) and *Waterloo Bridge* (1940) before turning to films noir like *Undercurrent* (1946) and eventually action-adventure films like *Ivanhoe* (1952) and *Knights of the Round Table* (1953). During World War II, Taylor served as a US Navy Air Corps flying instructor.

THE SPORTING LIFE

Clark Gable gets into the swing of things as he hits some golf balls on his Encino ranch, late 1950s. The manly Gable stole hearts with his rugged good looks and personable charm in the 1930s. His appearance sans undershirt in Frank Capra's romantic comedy *It Happened One Night* (1934) resulted in a huge drop in undershirt sales across the country.

THE SPORTING LIFE

Attractive young Marilyn Monroe prepares to tee off from the practice green at Riviera Golf Club in Los Angeles, early 1950s. Bombshell Monroe rocketed to superstardom thanks to her curvaceous body and sensual on-screen personality in such films as *Gentlemen Prefer Blondes* (1953), *There's No Business Like Show Business* (1954), and *The Seven Year Itch* (1955). She was married for nine months to baseball legend Joe DiMaggio and, later, for five years to renowned American playwright Arthur Miller.

THE SPORTING LIFE

A concentrating Kirk Douglas prepares to whack some practice balls at the Douglas Country Club during the making of the Korean War drama *The Hook* (1963). The film tells the story of two American privates ordered by their intense sergeant to kill an enemy airman they had captured. The manly Douglas, known for throwing himself into his parts, played tortured characters like Vincent Van Gogh in *Lust for Life* (1956) and Col. Dax. in *Paths of Glory* (1957).

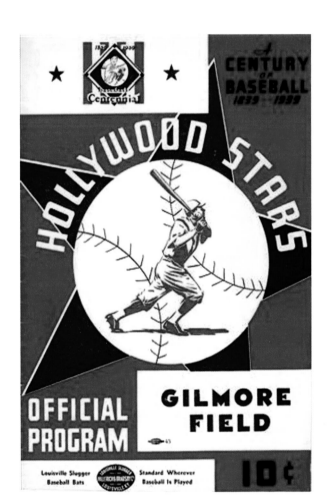

A CENTURY OF BASEBALL 1839 - 1939

HOLLYWOOD STARS

OFFICIAL PROGRAM

GILMORE FIELD

Louisville Slugger
Baseball Bats

Standard Wherever
Baseball Is Played

10¢

Sunset
BOWLING CENTER
The Bowling Showplace of the World

52 **LANES** 52

Hollywood Recreation..

SUNSET BOWLING CENTER

(52)

In the heart of Hollywood, open 24 hours a day . . .

World Famous 52 Lanes . . .

Cocktail lounge, serving the finest beverages. Cafe service par excellence . . .

Has been in existence eleven years, and an estimated nine million lines have been bowled on its glistening 52 lanes . . .

Phone for reservations—GLadstone 1146

SUNSET BOWLING CENTER IS . . .

The Bowling Showplace of the World!

5842 Sunset Boulevard
Hollywood, Calif.

Demure Irene Dunne practices a little golf between shots on the set of *The White Cliffs of Dover* (1944). A serious golfer, Dunne played Pebble Beach and many other courses, always hoping to conquer the golf course just as she did movie cameras. Hollywood discovered her thanks to her gorgeous singing voice before realizing what a wonderful actress she was as well. She starred in such films as *Show Boat* (1936), *The Awful Truth* (1937), *Love Affair* (1939), and *My Favorite Wife* (1940). In 1957, President Dwight D. Eisenhower appointed her as a special delegate to the United Nations.

An avid gun enthusiast and collector, Charlton Heston checks out a high-end scoped bolt action rifle. Charlton Heston was an iconic American actor and political activist for civil rights and the Second Amendment. During his sixty-year career as an actor he appeared in some of Hollywood's biggest box-office hits. Some of his most memorable roles include Moses in *The Ten Commandments* (1956), for which he was nominated for a Golden Globe Award, and his starring role in *Ben-Hur* (1959), for which he received the Academy Award for Best Actor.

Actor Don Ameche checks the double barrels of his shotgun during a day of bird hunting. Popular American actor and voice artist Ameche got his start on the vaudeville stage. In 1946 he took his interest in sports to a whole new level when he invested in a football team with fellow entertainment industry members that included Bing Crosby, Bob Hope, and Louis B. Mayer. The Los Angeles Dons were members of the now defunct All-America Football Conference that played their home games in the Los Angeles Memorial Coliseum, which they shared with the LA Rams. The team lasted until 1949 when it merged with the National Football League.

Ginger Rogers and William Boyd take a break from a midway shooting gallery while filming *Carnival Boat* (1932). The year 1932 was the beginning of trouble for Boyd's career. RKO Pictures canceled his contract in 1933 when his picture was mistakenly printed in a newspaper article about an actor with a similar name, William "Stage" Boyd, who had been arrested. The case of mistaken identity left him unemployed and near broke. However, for actress Ginger Rogers, a career was just beginning. Her success in the role of Anytime Annie in *42nd Street* (1933) caught the attention of RKO Radio Pictures and would lead to her pairing with Fred Astaire in a series of popular dance musicals.

Actor Ricardo Montalban shows off his superior athletic skills during a break in training for *Right Cross* (1950), a film set in the world of boxing. Montalban projected the sensuality and sophistication of the "Latin Lover" in Hollywood during the late 1940s and early 1950s. He showed his versatility as an actor in a series of films at M-G-M including *On an Island with You* (1948), *Border Incident* (1949), *Battleground* (1949), *Mystery Street* (1950), and *Across the Wide Missouri* (1951). And his biggest career success came in 1977 when he was cast as Mr. Roarke in the highly rated TV series *Fantasy Island* that ran until 1984.

A young and lanky Clint Eastwood performs a set of curls as part of a regular weight-lifting routine. While a contract player at Universal Pictures in the 1950s, Eastwood's physique was fine-tuned with the advice and supervision of professional bodybuilder, nutritionist, and early personal trainer Vince "Iron Guru" Gironda. Vince's San Fernando Valley location made it conveniently close to the studios of Warner Bros., Revue, Walt Disney, and Universal Pictures. Vince's Gym opened in 1948 and was a modest, no-frills, no-nonsense, old-school establishment for serious weight training only.

George Hamilton pumps some iron to keep in shape and reduce the stress of movie stardom. Hamilton learned the value of personal fitness at an early age. He grew up in a small town where the town doctor happened to be his grandfather. As a boy, he followed his grandfather on house calls to learn the facts about good health. He made sunbathing part of his health regimen once the girls started to take notice. Hamilton follows the advice of many health experts on the subjects of nutrition, cellular therapy, and caloric restriction.

WCF-P6

W. C. Fields breaks a sweat getting "back" in shape for the starring role in Universal Pictures *The Bank Dick* (1940). Fields began his show business career on the vaudeville stage. Ironically, as an entertainer now known for his sharp wit, he gained international stardom as a silent juggler. After a string of box-office hits for Paramount Pictures, Fields became a radio sensation sparring with Edgar Bergen on *The Chase and Sanborn Hour*. His ratings success led to a multipicture deal with Universal Pictures. Fields often tangled with studio executives, directors, and scriptwriters over creative control, always insisting on doing things his way.

M-G-M contract players Joan Crawford and Spencer Tracy take a break from a rigorous game of polo at the Will Rogers Ranch. Polo was a popular sport for Hollywood movers and shakers in the 1930s and '40s, and the most popular place to play was at the Will Rogers estate. It was a rustic retreat situated on over 180 acres, featuring horse corrals and stables, polo fields, and panoramic views of Beverly Hills and Pacific Palisades. Polo players here often included movie mogul Darryl Zanuck, Douglas Fairbanks, Clark Gable, Walt Disney, Gary Cooper, Tyrone Power, David Niven, and Tim Holt. After a long day on the field the gang would stop for refreshments at the Beverly Hills Hotel restaurant, which led to the restaurant being named the Polo Lounge.

THE SPORTING LIFE

Ready for action with mallet in hand, George Brent sits tall in the saddle atop his polo pony. Brent toured with a production of *Abie's Irish Rose* and acted with stock companies in Colorado, Rhode Island, Florida, and Massachusetts before appearing on Broadway in *Love, Honor, and Betray* with Clark Gable in 1930. In 1932, he signed a contract with Warner Bros., where he would remain for the next twenty years, becoming an A-list leading man during the late 1930s and 1940s. While at the Burbank studio it was rumored he had a two-year-long affair with frequent co-star Bette Davis, with whom he made eleven feature films.

An athletic Charles Farrell poses with his polo pony before the games begin. Farrell and fellow actor Ralph Bellamy opened the Racquet Club resort in Palm Springs, California, in December 1934. The club's original layout featured two tennis courts but would soon add additional courts, a swimming pool, and private bungalows. The Hollywood crowd used the Racket Club's "Bamboo Room" bar as a location for countless parties. The bar hosted an annual, jam-packed New Year's Eve party that was the desert "in" spot to celebrate the holiday.

Football players Lucille Ball and Gertie Green pose for publicity photos promoting Columbia's *Three Little Pigskins* in 1934. *Three Little Pigskins* was the fourth in a series of short subjects produced by Columbia Pictures and starring The Three Stooges, the slapstick comedy team of Moe Howard, Larry Fine, and Curly Howard. Also cast was a young blond-haired bit player named Lucille Ball in one of her earliest film roles. The stadium was a multipurpose, eighteen-thousand seater built by Earl Gilmore in Los Angeles, California. It became the first home for professional football in the City of Angels and hosted midget-car racing, and the property also housed Gilmore Field, the home of Hollywood Stars baseball team.

A young Marilyn Monroe poses for a cheesecake pinup photo as she hits the slopes in a two-piece swimsuit. In late 1944 the US Army Air Force's First Motion Picture Unit (FMPU) sent photographer David Conover to shoot morale-boosting pictures of female factory workers. Among the factory workers he met was a young Norma Jean Mortenson. None of her pictures were used by the FMPU, but Conover encouraged her to pursue a career in modeling. Heeding his advice, she signed with the Blue Book Model Agency. To get more work, she changed her hair from brunette and curly to blond and straight, and selected the professional name of Jean Norman.

William Boyd and Veronica Lake night ski on fresh winter snow in New York City's Central Park. Although Boyd was offered the supporting role of Red Connors in the 1935 movie *Hop-Along Cassidy*, he wanted the title role and got it. The *Hop-Along Cassidy* movies were produced with high-end production values, making them popular in urban and rural theaters. A has-been to many in the industry by 1948, Boyd was smart enough to buy the rights to all sixty-six of the *Hop-Along Cassidy* movies, eventually licensing prints of the series to NBC. Boyd's high stakes gamble paid off in spades, making him wealthier than ever before.

On the beach for one of her Wild-Muscle-Beach-Bikini-Blanket-Bingo-Party movies, Annette Joanne Funicello poses with her classic "signature" surfboard. During the early 1960s, American International Films approached Annette Funicello with the plan to feature the popular young actress in a low-budget teenage "sun and fun on the beach" movie. The producers reasoned that her large fan base of young males and females would help to guarantee an audience. However, before they could start production they needed Walt Disney to agree to a "loan out" because Annette was under contract to him. It was rumored that Disney gave his consent, with the provision that her navel always be covered-up by a one-piece bathing suit.

THE SPORTING LIFE

Like many a young Southern California native, Joel McCrea mastered the waves of the Pacific Ocean surfing with an old-school longboard. McCrea was born in South Pasadena, California, the son of an executive with the LA Gas & Electric Company. A paper route delivering copies of the *Los Angeles Times* to Cecil B. DeMille and other members of the film industry exposed him to the movies at a young age. McCrea found work as an extra, stunt man, and bit player, which eventually led to a contract with M-G-M, where he was cast in *The Jazz Age* (1929) and was given his first leading role in *The Silver Horde* (1930).

Wearing classic tennis "whites," Warner Baxter returns a volley with a perfectly formed backhand shot. Baxter's interest in show business started at an early age. With a display of entrepreneurial flair, he discovered a young boy who lived a block away who would eat worms and swallow flies for a penny. Baxter exhibited him in a makeshift tent and shared in 33 percent of the profits. Baxter received the Academy Award for Best Actor for his role as the Cisco Kid in the movie *In Old Arizona* (1928). Baxter had become the highest paid actor in Hollywood by 1936; he made over one hundred films between 1914 and 1950.

Shirley Temple and Guy Madison shake hands after an invigorating game of tennis during the filming of *Since You Went Away* (1944). Temple was, without question, the most popular and famous child movie star of all time, starting at the tender age of three. And by the age of five she could act, sing, and dance with the best and biggest names in the industry. Her cheery, can-do attitude helped America survive the Great Depression. The roles started to diminish as she transformed from a child to a preteen, and she made her last movie at the age of twenty-two. The career of Guy Madison (born Robert Moseley) started in 1944 on liberty from the US Navy in Hollywood during WWII. He was seated in the audience for a Lux Radio Theatre broadcast and was spotted by an assistant to David O. Selznick. Selznick was looking for an unknown sailor to play a small but prominent part in his production of *Since You Went Away* (1944) and signed Moseley to a contract.

Hoofer Fred Astaire shows off his well-known physical prowess as he leaps to return a high shot during a tennis rally. Astaire's elegant personal style was legendary; often creating his own signature looks, including once successfully using a necktie for a belt as a unique fashion statement. When his movie career waned he turned to television and made four highly rated and critically acclaimed television specials. Still spry at the advanced age of seventy-eight, he broke his left wrist riding his grandson's skateboard.

OUT AND ABOUT

Muscular hunk Robert Mitchum enjoys a little free time riding his bicycle along the pier, circa 1948. The handsome, sleepy-eyed Mitchum appeared in small roles in the early 1940s before gaining major stardom in such classic film noirs as *The Locket* (1946), *Crossfire* (1947), and *Out of the Past* (1947). Charismatic and laconic, his nonchalant style and "bad boy" personality attracted men and women alike.

Va-va-va-voom Annette Funicello zips along the beach carrying her surfboard on a Tule Trooper scooter, circa 1965. Rising to fame as one of the most popular Mouseketeers on Walt Disney's *Mickey Mouse Club* in the 1950s, Funicello stole teenage boys' hearts in the mid-1960s playing *Beach Blanket Bingo* with Frankie Avalon. Their series of beach party movies featured singing, dancing, surfing, and a little slapstick.

Richard Burton and Barbara Rush cruise around a New England harbor during a little downtime while making *The Bramble Bush* (1960). One of the first films to deal with euthanasia, the movie tells the story of a doctor (Burton) who returns to his New England home to help a suffering friend die. Haunted by his friend's death and his past, Burton finds solace in the arms of several female residents. Respected British stage actor Burton found acclaim in films in *My Cousin Rachel* (1952) and *The Robe* (1953) and would fall in love with actress Elizabeth Taylor during the making of *Cleopatra* (1963). Patrician Rush starred in such diverse 1950s films as *It Came from Outer Space* (1953), *Magnificent Obsession* (1954), and *Bigger Than Life* (1956) before adding popular TV series and TV movies to her résumé.

Sexy, young married couple Janet Leigh and Tony Curtis enjoy a leisurely sail around the lake in a colorful speedboat, circa 1955, soaking up sun. Parents of 1980s scream queen Jamie Lee Curtis, the dashing couple became movie stars in the 1940s thanks to their good looks and charming personalities. Leigh starred in such films as *Little Women* (1949) and *The Naked Spur* (1953) before gaining screen immortality in such movie classics as *Touch of Evil* (1958) and *Psycho* (1960). Curtis became a superstar after appearing in such hits as *Sweet Smell of Success* (1957), *The Defiant Ones* (1958), *Some Like It Hot* (1959), and *Spartacus* (1960).

Young beefcake Chad Everett and his dog drive around in Everett's snazzy Shelby Cobra convertible, early 1960s. The last actor ever under contract to the great motion picture studio M-G-M, Everett is most remembered for playing Dr. Joe Gannon in the TV series *Medical Center*. He appeared in films and television shows for several decades, including *Hawaiian Eye*, *The Dakotas,* and *Murder, She Wrote.*

A sparkly Rita Hayworth prepares to cut a pie to serve to American servicemen in the Hollywood Canteen, circa 1943. Born Margarita Cansino, the long-legged redhead worked as a dancer with her family until striking it big in such films as *The Strawberry Blonde* (1941), *You'll Never Get Rich* (1941), and *Cover Girl* (1944). She oozed sexual charisma in *Gilda* (1946) and in *The Lady from Shanghai* (1947), in which she starred with her husband, director Orson Welles.

Actor Alan Ladd and son David Ladd impress children's hero Roy Rogers with his new cowboy outfit and mask. The role of a hit man with a conscience in the 1942 adaptation of Graham Greene's novel *This Gun for Hire* made Alan Ladd a star at Paramount Studios. The film typecast him as a polished tough guy with a heart, a character he would go on to play in a series of successful films noir and Westerns. Roy Rogers was known as the "King of the Cowboys" at Republic Pictures starting in 1938, but he got his start singing with the musical act Sons of the Pioneers. He starred in feature Westerns, and his *The Roy Rogers Show* was popular on radio (1944–1955) and television (1951–1964). David Ladd would become a respected child actor before developing a lucrative career as a motion-picture and television producer.

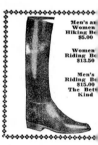

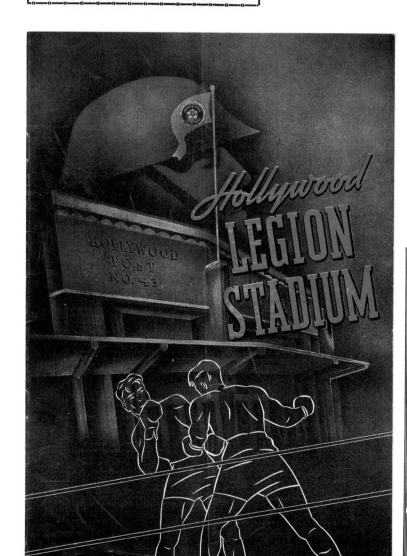

HOLLYWOOD
POST
NO. 43

Hollywood!
LEGION
STADIUM

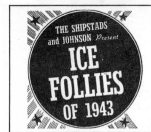

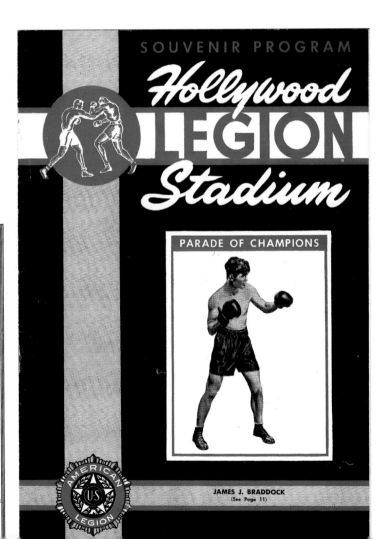

SOUVENIR PROGRAM

Hollywood **LEGION** *Stadium*

PARADE OF CHAMPIONS

JAMES J. BRADDOCK
(See Page 11)

Jane Powell hugs a trolley-pulling draft horse during a well-deserved trip to "the happiest place on earth," Disneyland in Anaheim, California. Jane Powell's professional career started in the summer of 1943, when her parents, Paul and Eileen Burce, took her on a vacation from hometown Portland, Oregon, to Hollywood, California. While in Hollywood, she appeared on Janet Gaynor's CBS radio talent show, *Hollywood Showcase: Stars over Hollywood*, sponsored by Ben Hur Coffee. Powell not only won the competition, but she also got the opportunity to audition for movie moguls David O. Selznick and M-G-M's Louis B. Mayer.

While backstage at the York Playhouse, a jubilant Lena Horne hugs her daughter, Gail Jones, after Jones made her triumphant stage debut in the opening performance of the musical *Valmouth* on October 7, 1960. Lena Horne got her first stage job at sixteen, dancing and later singing at the famed Cotton Club in Harlem, a renowned theater that featured black performers playing to mostly white audiences. Starting out as a member of the club's chorus line, she had the good fortune to be mentored by big established talents like jazz singer Adelaide Hall and bandleaders Cab Calloway and Duke Ellington. With their guidance and her natural talent, she became a popular musical star in her own right.

The Marx Brothers and theater owner Sid Grauman pose in Scottish kilts to mock the new trend in women's fashion of wearing slacks, prior to their hand-and-footprint ceremony in front of Grauman's Chinese Theatre on February 19, 1933. The famous Hollywood tradition located in the forecourt of Grauman's Chinese Theatre allegedly began when silent star Norma Talmadge accidentally stepped on the wet cement in front of the theater. During their ceremony the Marx Brothers left behind the imprint of Groucho's famous cigar. This was not the only unique variation to the traditional handprints and footprints ritual: Harold Lloyd left an imprint of his eyeglasses, John Barrymore left an imprint of his profile, Betty Grable left the imprint of her leg, and Sonja Henie left an imprint of her ice skate.

SAM GOLDWYN

Occupying Samuel Goldwyn's personal box, Douglas Fairbanks Jr., Tom Mix, Douglas Fairbanks, and George Raft attend the Hollywood Derby at Hollywood Park in Inglewood, California. Hollywood Park Racetrack was the original home of the Hollywood Derby, a Grade I American thoroughbred horse race held annually in late November/early December. The park would become one of Hollywood's favorite places to "play" and wager on "the Sport of Kings." The track was opened with great fanfare on June 10, 1938, by the Hollywood Turf Club. Warner Bros. movie mogul Jack Warner was the club's chairman. The 238-acre horse racing site could accommodate up to ten thousand spectators. Known as the "track of lakes and flowers," a unique feature of the park included an artificial lake in the center of the track.

A joyful James Stewart and wife Gloria, wearing straw hats and layers of tropical native flower leis, perfectly illustrate the traditional Hawaiian Islands greeting. James Stewart had a noted aviation career in the military, was a veteran of World War II and the Vietnam War, and obtained the rank of brigadier general in the US Air Force Reserve. A playboy bachelor and onetime roommate of lifelong friend Henry Fonda, he met the love of his life, Gloria Hartrich McLean, after his WWII military service. They married in 1949 and became one of Hollywood's happiest couples with a marriage that lasted forty-five years until her death in 1994.

OUT AND ABOUT

As his transatlantic journey on the *Queen Mary* comes to an end, Cary Grant films a home movie of the ship docking at a New York harbor in 1947. Grant was born in Horfield, Bristol, England, and lived in Los Angeles for most of his life. He made several pilgrimages to his homeland and was a frequent world traveler, often going from Southampton, England, to New York by ocean liner. It was while he was traveling first class to New York on the *Queen Mary* that he met his third wife, Betsy Drake, after asking actress friend Merle Oberon for an introduction.

ABOUT THE AUTHORS

Donovan Brandt is the owner and operator of Eddie Brandt's Saturday Matinee and has contributed to numerous Hollywood themed books and documentaries. He lives in North Hollywood.

Mary Mallory is a respected researcher, author, film historian, and author of *Hollywood Celebrates the Holidays* (2015), *Hollywoodland: Tales Lost and Found* (2013), and *Hollywoodland* (2011) and blogs for the *L.A. Daily Mirror*.

Stephen X. Sylvester is a filmmaker, preservationist, lecturer, and coauthor of *M-G-M: Hollywood's Greatest Backlot* (2011) and *Twentieth Century Fox: A Century of Entertainment* (Taylor Trade Publishing, 2016).